Analogue Guide

London

Rush
Library
Ph: 8708414

2nd Edition

Contents

London
—Welcome to Analogue London

London has played a significant role in world affairs to a greater or lesser extent since it was founded as a Roman settlement in the year 50, a long time ago even by English standards. As capital of the British Empire on which the sun famously never set, Victorian London was chosen as the baseline for international time conventions, making it quite literally the centre of the world. Subsequent decades of relative decline eventually gave way to the rise of "Cool Britannia" in the 1990s, and the opening of its borders to talent from across the globe.

Today, London is arguably the most international global city, and one in three Londoners was born abroad. Many feared the end of the good life when the money-spinning City stumbled in 2008, but the crisis had little impact on London's attraction to newcomers. Aside from its traditional connections to the Commonwealth, and its more recent favour among the worldwide oligarchy, London has also turned into somewhat of a *euro*-melting pot—quite a feat in a country that for centuries has defined itself against the madness of affairs on the Continent.

No Londoner worth his salt would ever admit to anything more than merely "quite liking it", but it would be hard to imagine a city as multifaceted not offering something new and inspiring for everyone—from the convivial pubs of Clerkenwell and the recent influx of Iberian and Antipodean influences on the culinary scene, to the cutting edge art and design of the East End and the ideal of postcard pretty Notting Hill.

We've aspired to unearth the best of all of this, with photographs and maps throughout. Enjoy!

Neighbourhoods

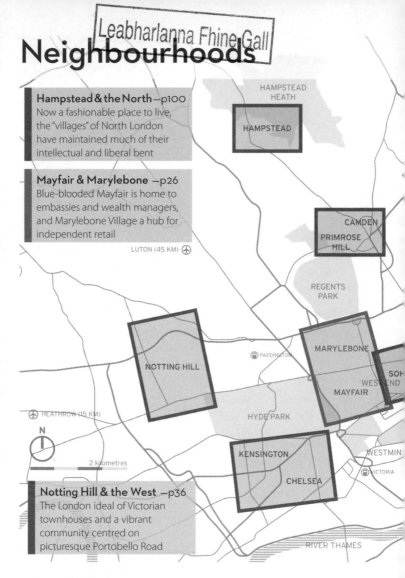

Leabharlanna Fhine Gall

Hampstead & the North —p100
Now a fashionable place to live, the "villages" of North London have maintained much of their intellectual and liberal bent

Mayfair & Marylebone —p26
Blue-blooded Mayfair is home to embassies and wealth managers, and Marylebone Village a hub for independent retail

LUTON (45 KM) ⊕

HAMPSTEAD HEATH

HAMPSTEAD

CAMDEN

PRIMROSE HILL

REGENTS PARK

⊕ PADDINGTON

MARYLEBONE

NOTTING HILL

SOH

WEST END

MAYFAIR

⊕ HEATHROW (15 KM)

HYDE PARK

N

2 kilometres

KENSINGTON

WESTMIN

VICTORIA

CHELSEA

Notting Hill & the West —p36
The London ideal of Victorian townhouses and a vibrant community centred on picturesque Portobello Road

RIVER THAMES

Soho & Covent Garden —p8
London's urban core is packed with restaurants, bars, retail and entertainment, and what remains of its less salubrious past

Clerkenwell & Islington —p68
A former light manufacturing hub and left-wing print shop, the area's lofts and terraces are now home to media and advertising types

Shoreditch & the East —p50
The East End has morphed into an interesting hotchpotch of its down heeled past and its reincarnation as the city's new artistic epicentre

✈ STANSTED (45 KM)

ISLINGTON

ST PANCRAS

CLERKENWELL

BETHNAL GREEN

SHOREDITCH

🚇 LIVERPOOL ST

CENT
DEN

THE CITY

CITY AIRPORT (5 KM) ✈

SOUTH BANK

BERMONDSEY

CANARY WHARF

South Bank —p86
Historically lagging London proper in urbanity, the Thames' southern banks are today a cultural and epicurean highlight

✈ GATWICK (35 KM)

Soho & Covent Garden
—24-Hour Urban Core

Soho has long held a reputation as the focal point of London's nightlife—from the theatres of the West End to the nightclubs off Old Compton and Dean Streets, to what remains of the area's heritage as a seedy red light district. Densely packed with restaurants, bars and coffee shops, Soho is the closest that London comes to a 24-hour city. The area is also a centre of creative and media businesses, notably from the film industry.

Despite early efforts to develop Soho along the lines of grander Mayfair and Bloomsbury, the area never caught on with the wealthy; those who could had moved out by the mid-18th century. Subsequent decades of immigration and neglect turned its streets into a hotbed of prostitution and artistry, shaping the quirky identity that Soho enjoys today. South of Shaftsbury Avenue, pedestrianised Gerrard Street is the heart of London's Chinatown. To the north, beneath the 1960s-glamour BT Tower, Fitzrovia is home to advertising agencies and architectural firms, along with an increasingly interesting array of culinary offerings.

Covent Garden, Soho's less brash sibling across the Charing Cross Road, has seen its fortunes tied to its fruit and vegetable market. The neoclassical market hall, erected in 1830, had outgrown its purposes by the 1960s, and the market was moved out. The neighbourhood became popular with new residents in the 1980s when the market hall re-opened as a shopping centre. Today, Covent Garden is a popular retail destination, with pockets of sophistication around Neil's Yard and the Seven Dials. To its north, the literary and academic enclave of Bloomsbury is the birthplace of literary modernism and home to the British Museum.

Edwardian Soho Revived

Dean Street Townhouse

1. 69-71 Dean St
+44 20 7434 1775
deanstreettownhouse.com
⊖⊖ Tottenham Court Road,
⊖⊖ Piccadilly Circus
Doubles from £175/night incl. tax

Dean Street Townhouse offers a slice of history in the thick of Soho without eschewing any of the warmth and luxury of a contemporary boutique hotel. Housed in the former Gargoyle Club, the haunt of artists the likes of Francis Bacon and Lucien Freud, the space was converted into a thirty-nine bedroom hotel in 2009. Located at the corner of gorgeous cobble-stoned Meard Street, the Townhouse is but a stone's throw from many of London's best restaurants, museums and entertainment.

Antipodean Coffee Highlight

Flat White

2 17 Berwick St
+44 20 7734 0370

flatwhitecafe.com

⊖⊖ Piccadilly Circus,
⊖⊖⊖ Oxford Circus

Open daily. Mon-Fri 8am-7pm; Sat/
Sun 9am-6pm

Flat White does antipodean coffee and brunch-on-the-go at its absolute best. The flat whites at this establishment are so smooth that even the most discerning connoisseur will gasp with delight at the first sip. Grab a table amidst the local media types, delve into a copy of one of the design magazines on offer and indulge in a toasted banana bread slice or some scrambled eggs. Flat White's sister establishment Milkbar, located a few blocks away, is equally enticing.

Nordic Café

Nordic Bakery

③ 14a Golden Sq
+44 20 3230 1077
nordicbakery.com
⊖⊖ Piccadilly Circus
Open daily. Mon-Fri 8am-8pm; Sat
9am-7pm; Sun 10am-7pm

One of the most serene spots in central London, Nordic Bakery is a haven for fresh baked Nordic delicacies, such as warm *kanelbulle* and *smörgås* open-faced sandwiches, served up alongside excellent espresso based drinks. The Golden Square location is bang in the middle of Soho and patrons include media types stopping in for a break from the surrounding creative offices. Floor to ceiling windows allow for unique views of Soho life and the interior design is dotted with elements by Alvar Aalto, Kaj Franck and Ilmari Tapiovaara.

Coffee & Charcuterie

Fernandez & Wells

4 43 Lexington St
+44 20 7734 1546
fernandezandwells.com
◒◒◒ Oxford Circus,
◒◒ Piccadilly Circus
Open daily. Mon-Fri 11am-10pm; Sat/
Sun noon-10pm
Beak Street: Mon-Fri 7.30am-6pm;
Sat 9am-6pm; Sun 9am-10pm

Fernandez & Wells' fabulous quartet of locations specialise in the best of British and continental produce in a resolutely English setting. Nestled on quaint Lexington Street, this branch features a sumptuous spread of delights—so whether it's a thirty-six month cured *jamón ibérico de bellota* sandwich drizzled with olive oil or a sip of premium sherry you're after, you will find it in its absolute finest form at Fernandez & Wells.

Coffee Pioneer

Monmouth Café

27 Monmouth St
+44 20 7232 3010
monmouthcoffee.co.uk
⊖ Covent Garden, ⊖ ⊖ Tottenham Court Road
Closed Sun. Mon-Sat 8am-6.30pm

Roasting and retailing beans since 1978, Monmouth's original café location in the heart of Covent Garden's Seven Dials area serves decadently strong single cone filter coffee, espresso based drinks and a staggering array of pastries in a warm and convivial setting. The tiny space is decked out with rough slabs of wood and the aroma of freshly ground coffee percolates every corner. Monmouth's Borough Market (p91) location allows patrons to soak up the bucolic atmosphere of the surrounding market stalls.

Yoga Studio

triyoga

6 Kingly Court, 2nd Floor
+44 20 7483 3344

triyoga.co.uk

⊖⊖⊖ Oxford Circus,
⊖⊖ Piccadilly Circus

Classes daily, refer to website for schedule. Drop-in classes from £13. Mats available free of charge

Triyoga offers a vast range of high quality yoga, pilates and gyrotonics classes, as well as scores of treatments to complement one's practice. Atypical for its central London location, the Soho branch offers ample studio space, complete with charming views of the panoply of surrounding central London rooftops. The Primrose Hill location (map p103) also boasts a relaxing café.

Fashion & Design Temple

Liberty

7 Great Marlborough St
+44 20 7734 1234
liberty.co.uk
⊖⊖⊖ Oxford Circus
Open daily. Mon-Sat 10am-8pm; Sun noon-6pm

Arthur Liberty's design emporium has been at the forefront of home wares and fashion since its inception in 1875. The store's colourful history is reflected in the magnificent Art Nouveau designs it pioneered in the 1920s. The founder's vision propelled him to travel the globe to source exquisite artefacts and fabrics to put on display in his ever-expanding central London outlet. Today, Liberty's famously mock tudor shop remains at the vanguard of fashion and design and is a highlight of the London shopping circuit.

Udon Specialist

Koya

 49 Frith St
+44 20 7434 4463

koya.co.uk

⊖⊖ Tottenham Court Road
Open daily. Mon-Sat noon-3pm,
5.30pm-10.30pm; Sun noon-3pm,
5.30pm-10pm

Koya offers the chance to indulge in a top-notch bowl of homemade Udon noodles in an unruffled and welcoming setting. The simple, bright dining room merges wood with tile, and the bar area at the rear allows for a behind-the-scenes glimpse into the creation process of Udon. Dishes range from Atsu-Atsu (hot noodle with hot broth) to Hiya-Hiya (cold noodle with cold sauce) and the combined cold-hot delight known as Hiya-Atsu—all in several different incarnations. For those on the run, head to Koya Bar next door, which spins out a smashing repertoire at its long Japanese-style noodle and rice bar.

Seasonally Driven French

Ducksoup

 41 Dean St
+44 20 7287 4599
ducksoupsoho.co.uk
⊖⊖ Tottenham Court Road,
⊖⊖ Piccadilly Circus
Open daily. Mon-Sat noon-midnight;
kitchen closes at 10.30pm; Sun
1pm-6pm

Dean Street's latest foodie haunt,
trendy but intimate Ducksoup
takes its inspiration from France's
neighbourhood restaurants. The
innovative wine list focuses on
natural and biodynamic selections
form a handfull of small producers
and the seasonally driven menu
is hand written daily. At night, sit
at the long bar and enjoy service
directly from the chef.

Great British Cuisine

Great Queen Street

10 32 Great Queen St
+44 20 7242 0622

⊖⊖ Holborn

Open daily. Mon-Sat noon-2.30pm,
6pm-10.30pm; Sun 1pm-4pm

This charmingly discrete and dimly lit restaurant at the fringes of Covent Garden offers outstanding fresh seasonal fare, artfully whipped into modern British classics. Great Queen Street's sophisticated menu, wine list and clientele add luster and flair to a neighbourhood generally associated with retail therapy. The imposing art deco Freemason's Hall across the street is a sight to behold.

Oysters & Champagne

Randall and Aubin

11 16 Brewer St
+44 20 7287 4447
randallandaubin.com
⊖⊖ Piccadilly Circus
Open daily. Mon-Wed noon-11pm;
Thu-Sat noon-midnight; Sun noon-
10pm

Randall & Aubin is a celebratory space, drawing in Soho's crackling energy, while revelling in its own discrete panache. The ultimate spot to crack open a bottle of champagne to marry with oysters or any of the other seafood and charcuterie on offer. The site of the restaurant was originally a butcher specialising in the best of Paris and British produce. Inspired by these roots, Randall & Aubin's menu reflects the space's heritage with stellar results.

Convivial Tapas Bar

Barrafina

12 54 Frith St
+44 20 7813 8016
barrafina.co.uk
⊖⊖ Tottenham Court Road
Open daily. Mon-Sat noon-3pm,
5pm-11pm; Sun 1pm-3.30pm,
5.30pm-10pm

Located in the throbbing core of
Frith Street, Barrafina soaks in all the
local pizazz while retaining uniquely
nonchalant but perennially
fashionable flair. Tapas are incredibly
fresh and artfully prepared and the
wine list is excellent. So take a seat
at the marble bar, indulge in that
jamón de jabugo with a scintillating
glass of Verdejo from Rueda and
mingle with the crowd.

Independent Film and Drinks

Curzon Cinema

13 99 Shaftesbury Av
+44 330 500 1331
curzoncinemas.com
⊖⊖ Leicester Square
Screenings daily. Refer to website
for showtimes
Tickets £12.50

The Curzon group's five cinemas, scattered throughout London, screen the best of contemporary film. The Curzon Soho also boasts a lively street-side Konditor & Cook café, serving delightful pastries alongside frothy cappuccinos. The popular full bar downstairs makes an experience at this bastion of international independent and arthouse cinema refreshingly unique.

Mayfair & Marylebone

—Blue Blooded and Quintessentially English

Grand yet understated, Mayfair is the quintessentially English centre of aristocratic London life. Less residential that it once was, its magnificent Edwardian and Georgian real estate now houses embassies, wealth managers and hedge funds, as well as some of London's most exclusive boutiques. Marylebone, no less aristocratic in its heritage, but arguably more democratic in feel, has become an interesting destination for independent retail.

Well-heeled from the outset and situated just adjacent to the expanses of Hyde Park, Mayfair was originally developed as a fashionable residential district. To this day, the Duke of Westminster and the Grosvenor family own much of the underlying freehold land. As many of the neighbourhood's wealthy residents gravitated towards the leafy streets of Kensington, the area became the preferred corporate headquarters of Britain plc. Today, Mayfair is renowned for its high-end fashion and art scene, notably around Bond and Dover Streets, as well as the bespoke tailoring of Savile Row. The offerings of Mayfair itself stand in stark contrast to the predictable retail mix of Oxford Street and more elegant Regent Street, its boundaries to the north and east respectively.

Marylebone was commissioned by its landlords in the 18th century as a residential neighbourhood on a rational street grid. The neighbourhood long lived in the shadow of grander Mayfair. However, more recently the streets around Marylebone High Street, also known as Marylebone Village, have turned into an attractive hub for independent shops—not to an insignificant degree due to careful lease management by its landowner, the Howard de Walden Estate.

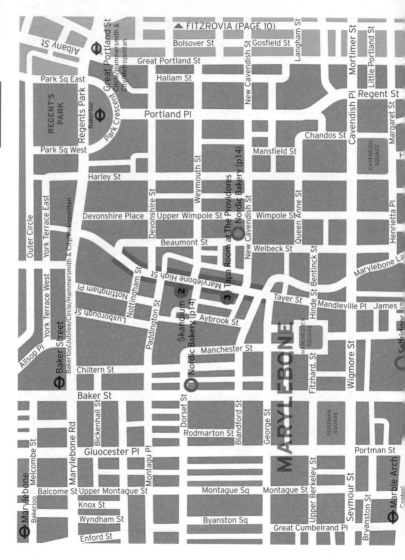

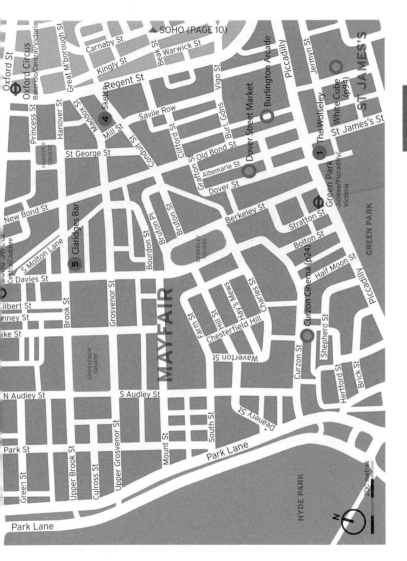

Piccadilly Splendour

The Wolseley

1 160 Piccadilly
+44 20 7499 6996
thewolseley.com
⊖⊖⊖ Green Park
Open daily. Mon-Fri 7am-midnight;
Sat 8am-midnight; Sun 8am-11pm

In the 1920s Wolseley Motors, now defunct, commissioned a grandiose car showroom on prestigious Piccadilly. While the car business did not fare all that well, The Wolseley was reborn in 2003 as one of the premier Continental-style café-restaurants in London. The bling of the setting and diverse clientele add to the celebratory exuberance of such delights as The Wolseley Champagne Tea, on offer daily.

Skandinavian Design

Skandium

2 88 Marylebone High St
+44 20 7935 2077
skandium.com
⊖⊖⊖⊖⊖ Baker Street
Open daily. Mon-Wed 10am-6.30pm;
Thu 10am-7pm; Fri/Sat 10am-
6.30pm; Sun 11am-5pm

Skandium does not seem too far off from its aim of being the best retailer of Scandinavian design and furniture in the world. Founded by a Finn, a Swede and a Dane, all involved in the design industry in some capacity, the store is a haven of Nordic clean lines, soft wood and gorgeous textiles. To add to the authenticity, you will surely hear Swedish being spoken on Marylebone High Street, as the neighbourhood has long been a favourite of expat Swedes living in the British capital.

Auckland Meets Marylebone

Tapa Room at
The Providores

 109 Marylebone High St
+44 20 7935 6175

theprovidores.co.uk

⊖⊖⊖⊖ Baker Street, ⊖⊖ Bond
Street

Open daily. Mon-Fri 9am-11.30am,
noon-10.30pm; Sat 9am-3pm, 4pm-
10.30pm; Sun 9am-3pm, 4pm-10pm

An exciting fusion restaurant specializing in small dishes and wine, The Tapa Room offers an unusually vast oenological selection originating from New Zealand's ten major wine regions. The restaurant's innovative culinary approach is complemented by an equally strong coffee culture. Tapa is named after the Pacific decorative rug adorning the space's most prominent wall.

Stylish Mayfair

Sketch

9 Conduit St
+44 20 7659 4500
sketch.uk.com
⊖⊖⊖ Oxford Circus
The Gallery: Open daily 6pm-midnight
The Parlour: Open daily. Mon-Fri 8am-2am; Sat 10am-2am; Sun 10am-midnight

Divided into five flamboyantly decorated dining rooms and bars, Sketch is more of an experience than a restaurant. From decadent afternoon tea at the front room Parlour to a multi-course tasting menu at the Michelin starred Lecture Room, the venue caters to every whim. The Gallery, Sketch's brasserie, offers an ever-changing set of giant video images created by emerging artists to complement your French inspired meal. The bathrooms upstairs, consisting of retro-futuristic giant individual egg-like pods, are otherworldly.

Classic Drinks

Claridge's Bar

5 49 Brook St
+44 20 7629 8860
claridges.co.uk
⊖⊖ Bond Street
Open daily. Mon-Sat noon-1am; Sun noon-midnight

A quintessential English classic, refined, elegant and understated, a cocktail at Claridges Bar is a must. The original art deco features, including red leather banquettes, are scrupulously maintained. The unfussy luxury of the establishment pairs perfectly with one of London's most extensive champagne lists.

Notting Hill & the West

—Leafy London Ideal

Notting Hill comes closest to the London ideal sought by visitors and Londoners alike: well-kept Victorian townhouses, colourful mews and expansive private communal gardens. The neighbourhood is a vibrant, artistic, and still fairly mixed community centred on the picturesque Portobello Road street market.

The hill near the *Nutting-barns* manor was largely rural until the early 19th century when local landlords laid out plans for a fashionable suburb to capitalize on London's westward expansion. However, as middle class households ceased to employ servants in the first half of the 20th century, the large Notting Hill houses lost their market, and by the late 1950s many buildings had turned into down-market slums. The area was one of the few London neighbourhoods where Afro-Caribbean immigrants could find housing in postwar London. Subsequent attempts at "urban renewal" have left their mark on the neighbourhood, most notably Ernő Goldfinger's (also see p105) famously stark Trellick Tower. Notting Hill was rediscovered by the middle classes in the 1980s and developed into the urban idyll so famously portrayed in the eponymous 1999 film.

Today no less gentrified than other parts of Kensington and Chelsea, Notting Hill has maintained some of its social variety and artistic affinity. A short walk from the imposing and elegant white townhouses near Notting Hill Gate, Westbourne Grove and Ledbury Road have developed a reputation for their upmarket boutiques and eateries. Portobello Road, home to the famous Portobello Market, leads to the neighbourhood's edgier parts at the bottom of the hill. Further beyond, North Kensington's Golborne Road still exudes the neighbourhood's artistic and immigrant spirit.

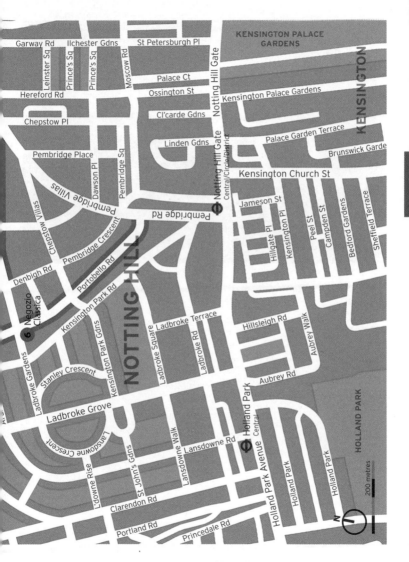

Notting Hill Brunch

Raoul's

(1) 105-107 Talbot Rd
+44 20 7229 2400
raoulsgourmet.com
Westbourne Park,
Notting Hill Gate
Open daily. Mon-Fri 7.30am-8pm; Sat
8.30am-8pm; Sun 8.30am-7pm

A Notting Hill brunch classic, Raoul's is a people watching paradise with a heated outside terrace to match. Combining Mediterranean cuisine with more classic brunch items, the menu is versatile around the clock. Cheerful yellow accents highlighting the blonde wooden tables and oversized mirrors make for a soothing and light ambiance. For those who prefer brunch on the go, Raoul's now boasts a lower ground floor take-away deli.

Neighbourhood Café

Teas Me

2 129a Ladbroke Grove
+44 20 7729 5577
⊖⊖ Ladbroke Grove
Closed Sun. Open Mon-Sat 8am-5.30pm

In a nod to the neighbourhood's lesser known Portuguese influences, Teas Me serves an excellent breakfast/brunch as well as an array of delectable homemade cakes, teas and coffees. The ambiance is warm, refined and convivial, and a newspaper strewn common table is meticulously decorated with fresh flowers. On warmer days tables are also set outside on Ladbroke Crescent, a picturesque cul-de-sac just off Ladbroke Grove.

Notting Hill Public House

The Westbourne

3 101 Westbourne Park Villas
+44 20 7221 1332
thewestbourne.com
⊖⊖ Royal Oak
Open daily. Mon-Wed 4.30pm-11pm;
Thu-Sat 11am-11pm; Sun noon-
10.30pm
Kitchen: Mon-Sat 6.30pm-10.15pm;
Sun 6.30pm-9.30pm
Lunch: Thu-Sun 12.30pm-3.30pm

An ever-popular gastropub on a Notting Hill corner bursting with wild flowers, The Westbourne serves a constantly changing menu chiselled out of locally sourced produce in a jovial setting. A good variety of wines and beers are on offer, and the Westbourne's generous terrace is one of London's best. For those wanting to stay inside during the colder months, the pub's interior is all warm tones and wood.

East Meets West

E&O

4 14 Blenheim Crescent
+44 20 7229 5454
rickerrestaurants.com
⊖⊖ Ladbroke Grove
Open daily. Mon-Fri noon-midnight;
Sat 11am-midnight; Sun 11am-11.30pm
Kitchen: Mon-Fri noon-3pm, 6pm-
11pm; Sat 11am-11pm; Sun 11am-
10.30pm

On a bijou corner of Blenheim
Crescent, E&O serves nouveau
pan-Asian cuisine in a modern,
urbane setting. Dishes are artfully
displayed and are matched by the
high calibre of the wine and drinks
list. Australian ownership makes for
a refreshingly laid back experience.
The front bar and outdoor benches
are stellar spots to quaff a cocktail
or two.

Boutique Cinema

The Electrica

⑤ 191 Portobello Rd
+44 20 7908 9696
electricbrasserie.com
⊖⊖ Ladbroke Grove,
⊖⊖⊖ Notting Hill Gate
Diner: Open daily. Mon-Wed 8am-midnight; Thu-Sat 8am-1am; Sun 8am-11pm
Screenings daily. Refer to website for showtimes
Tickets £18

London's most unusual and luxurious film house is happily combined with one of Notting Hill's most bustling restaurants. The Electric Cinema comes replete with oversized chairs, plush footrests and side tables on which to rest your glass of champagne and mixed olives. Those seeking more intimacy can opt for a double love seat. Combine the show with some Continentally inspired American fare at the adjoining diner, and enjoy the spectacle of Portobello Road as it unfolds before your eyes.

Italian Wine Bar

Negozio Classica

6 283 Westbourne Grove
+44 20 7034 0005
negozioclassica.co.uk
⊖⊖⊖ Notting Hill Gate
Open daily. Mon-Thu 3.30pm-
midnight; Fri/Sun 10am-midnight;
Sat 9am-midnight

A sleek Italian wine bar and café,
Negozio Classica offers the best
of Italy in the heart of Notting Hill.
The bar, comfy living room chairs
and discreet fireplaces conjure the
luxury of a Milanese lounge. Wines
can be paired with an epicurean
selection of cheeses and cured
meats and many of the items are
also available to purchase for later
consumption. During the day,
Negozio Classica lends itself very
well to the rapturous combination
of espresso and newspaper.

KENSINGTON

Royal Albert Hall

7 V&A Museum
Skandium (p31)

Natural History Museum

Gloucester Rd
Picadilly/District/Circle

Fernandez & Wells (p15)

South Kensington
Piccadilly/District/Circle

N
200 metres

Design Heritage

V&A Museum

7 Cromwell Rd
+44 20 7942 2000
vam.ac.uk
⊖⊖⊖ South Kensington
Open daily. Sat-Thu 10am-5.45pm;
Fri 10am-10pm
Free admission

A bastion of decorative arts and design, the Victoria & Albert Museum's sweeping collection of 4.5 million objects would be reason enough to visit, but the building's architecture provides motivation just as compelling. Founded in 1852, the museum's collection spans the globe and five thousand years of design. The V&A's focus is on practically used objects, rather than high art or research, thus offering fascinating insights into the visual history of the quotidian. Ever the trendsetter, the museum was the first in Britain to host a rock concert in 1973.

Chelsea Contemporary

Saatchi Gallery

(8) Duke of York's HQ, King's Road
+44 20 7811 3070
saatchigallery.com
⊖⊖ Sloane Square
Open daily 10am-6pm
Free admission

The Saatchi Gallery has been a pioneer of the global contemporary art world since Charles Saatchi opened his collection to the public in 1985. Launching the careers of scores of previously unknown—and several controversial—artists, the gallery first focused on American art, exhibiting the work of abstract expressionists and minimalists before segueing into its backing of Damien Hirst and the Young British Artists movement. Ever on the cusp of global trends, Saatchi's Duke of York's HQ off the King's Road in Chelsea opened in 2008 with an exhibition of New Chinese Art.

Shoreditch & the East

—London's Cutting Edge

Only two decades ago Shoreditch was a wasteland of light industrial structures on the fringes of the City of London, the old Roman settlement and today's financial district. All this changed in the 1990s when the area around Hoxton Square turned into the epicentre of a thriving art scene. When Hoxton's iconic White Cube gallery moved out in 2012, some mused that the area's artistic gravitas had given way to the juggernaut of an encroaching wave of hipster culture.

The East End, unlike London's western suburbs, did not see much planned development but grew as an impromptu response to London's breakneck expansion during the Industrial Revolution and the extension of the nearby docks. Spitalfields and Brick Lane in particular have been shaped by the waves of immigrants who lived there—Huguenots in the 17th century, Irish and Jewish, and more recently Bangladeshi. The narrow lanes of Jack the Ripper's 19th century East End fell victim to the air raids of the German Blitz during World War II, which turned swathes of terraces into rubble. The closure of London's docks in the 1980s added another setback, although this was partly offset by office developments that sprouted up at Canary Wharf in the 1990s.

The East End today has morphed into an interesting hotchpotch of its down-heeled past and its more buoyant present. The core of the former bohemian neighbourhood around Hoxton Square and Redchurch Street is now a mecca for trendy boutiques and upscale restaurants. The area near the Old Street roundabout is a centre of London's burgeoning tech start-up scene. To the south, Spitalfields Market has developed into an mainstream retail success story. Most artists have moved east to rough around the edges neighbourhoods beyond Bethnal Green.

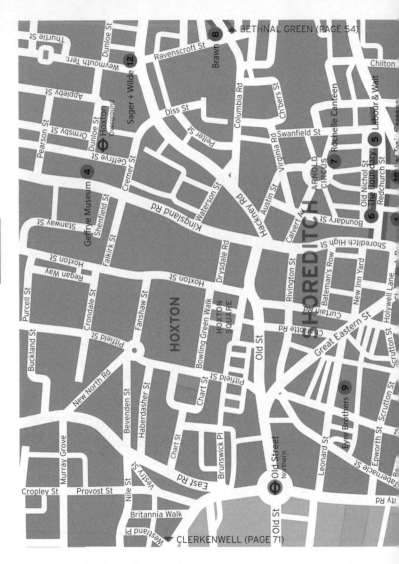

BETHNAL GREEN (PAGE 54)

Chilton

Thurtle St

Dunloe St

Weymouth Terr.

12

Ravenscroft St

Brawn 8

Appleby St

Diss St

Columbia Rd

Sager + Wilde

Pearson St

Ormsby St

Dunloe St

Hoxton Overground

Peller St

Ch'bers St

Swanfield St

Virginia Rd

Rachelle Canteen 7

Labour & Wait 5

Stanway St

Geffrye Museum 4

Shenfield St

Cremer St

Gettfrye St

Kingsland Rd

Waterson St

Austin St

ARNOLD CIRCUS

SHOREDITCH

Old Nichol St

The Boundary 6

Redchurch St

Falkirk St

Hoxton St

Hackney Rd

Calvert Av

Boundary St

Shoreditch High St

Regan Way

Purcell St

Crondale St

Fanshaw St

Drysdale Rd

Hoxton St

HOXTON

Rivington St

Bateman's Row

New Inn Yard

Buckland St

Pitfield St

Bowling Green Walk

HOXTON SQUARE

Old St

Curtain Rd

Charlotte Rd

Great Eastern St

Holywell Lane

New North Rd

Bevenden St

Haberdasher St

Chart St

Pitfield St

Chart St

Brunswick Pl

Scrutton St

Eyre Brothers 9

Scrutton St

Epworth St

Tabernacle St

Murray Grove

Nile St

Vestry St

East Rd

Leonard St

Cropley St

Provost St

Britannia Walk

Westland Pl

Old St

Old Street Northern

CLERKENWELL (PAGE 71)

ity Rd

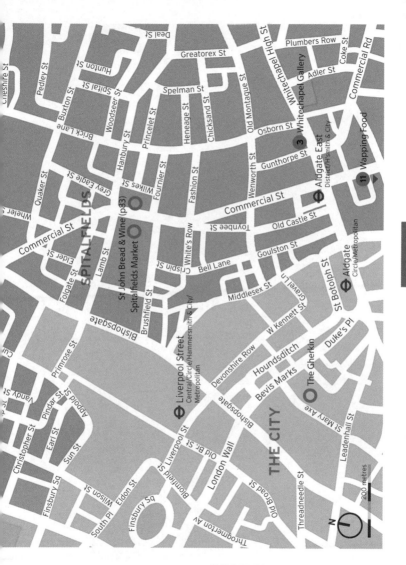

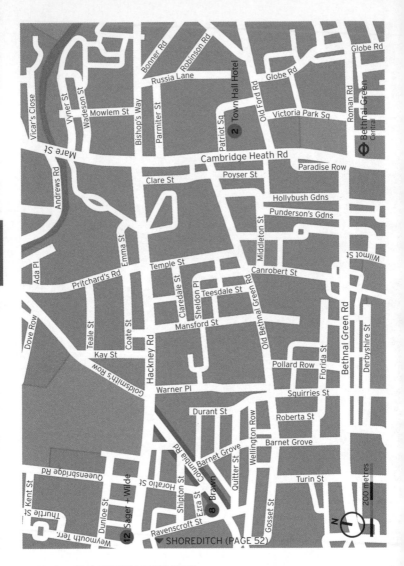

Shoreditch House Accommodation

Shoreditch Rooms

1 Ebor St
+44 20 7739 5040
shoreditchhouse.com
Shoreditch High Street,
Liverpool Street
Doubles from £165/night incl. tax

Shoreditch House is the East End offshoot of Soho House, the global members' club. The Shoreditch Rooms are open to non-members. Accommodation is spread over five floors of pleasantly airy rooms with vintage touches and sweeping views of the City or of charming Ebor Street. Smack in the middle of the East End's most vibrant neighbourhood, this is the place to be for a taste of contemporary London and some pampering, facilitated by the presence of the on-site Cowshed Spa and Gym.

Edwardian Glamour

Town Hall Hotel

2 Patriot Square
+44 20 7871 0460
townhallhotel.com
⊖ Bethnal Green
Doubles from £163/night incl. tax

Set in the borough's former town hall, the Town Hall Hotel brings a glamourous twist to Bethnal Green, one of the East End's more up-and-coming areas. The majestic structure was built in 1910, at the pinnacle of Edwardian architectural splendour, and Art Deco accents were added during an expansion in the 1930s. Meticulously restored with modern accents, the hotel's update won the prestigious RICS London award in 2011. Viajante, the hotel's restaurant and bar, is a gorgeous spot worthy of a trip East in of itself.

East End Pioneer
Whitechapel Gallery
3 77-82 Whitechapel High St
+44 20 7522 7888
whitechapelgallery.org
⊖⊖ Aldgate East, ⊖⊖ Aldgate
Closed Mon. Fri-Wed 11am-6pm; Thu
11am-9pm
Free admission

The Whitechapel Gallery focuses on modern and contemporary art in one of London's rough-around-the-edges neighbourhoods. In 1956, the gallery's "This Is Tomorrow" exhibition famously launched Pop Art as a popular genre. Thanks to the London Open, its open-submission show running since 1936, Whitechapel has catapulted the careers of several renowned artists, including sculptor Anish Kapoor. The gallery's downstairs dining room is minimalist chic, while the upstairs café with its thick wooden planks offers fresh and sprightly lunch specials.

London Homes throughout History

Geffrye Museum

(4) 136 Kingsland Rd
+44 20 7739 9893
geffrye-museum.org.uk
⊖ Hoxton
Closed Mon. Tue-Sun 10am-5pm
Free admission

The Geffrye Museum affords visitors a fascinating glimpse into the history of England's changing domestic interior design from the 1600s to the present. A series of eleven rooms serves to illustrate the different periods with typical furnishing, ornaments and wallpaper, supplemented by illuminating explanatory notes. In addition, the museum showcases four wildly varying English gardens, each one representing horticultural styles of the past four centuries.

Design Classics for the Home

Labour and Wait

5 85 Redchurch St
+44 20 7729 6253
labourandwait.co.uk
⊖ Shoreditch High Street,
⊖⊖⊖⊖ Liverpool Street
Closed Mon. Open Tue-Sun 11am-
6pm

Having grown weary of fast fashion's ravages, menswear design veterans Rachel Wythe-Moran and Simon Watkins developed the concept for Labour & Wait. With a focus on craftsmanship and timeless design, the shop's highly curated selection of functional objects never fails to delight. From Welsh blankets to English pottery, vintage flasks and Japanese enamel teapots joyfully displayed in the shop's inviting setting; you will be sure to unearth a treasure or two.

Hotel, Restaurant & Rooftop Bar

The Boundary Project

(6) 2-4 Boundary St
+44 20 7729 1051
theboundary.co.uk
⊖ Shoreditch High Street,
⊖⊖⊖⊖ Liverpool Street
Albion: Open daily 8am-11pm
Rooftop: Open daily. Mon-Fri noon-11.30pm; Sat/Sun 10am-11.30pm
Boundary Rooms: Doubles from £275/night incl. tax

The slick and contemporary Boundary Project by British design icon Terence Conran includes three restaurants, a hotel and a gallery space, but the jewel in the crown is surely the gorgeous outdoor rooftop bar and grill, now conveniently weather-proofed for year-round pleasure, complete with stunning views of London's East End and the City. The Albion Café on the ground floor serves top of the line British fare, some of which it also sells retail in its in-house shop.

Hidden Treasure
Rochelle Canteen

7 Arnold Circus
+44 20 7729 5677
arnoldandhenderson.com
⊖ Shoreditch High Street,
⊖⊖⊖⊖ Liverpool Street
Closed Sat/Sun. Open Mon-Fri
9am-11.30pm, noon-3pm (lunch),
3pm-4.30pm (tea)

Delicious, fresh lunches are served on weekdays in this urban oasis hidden in a Victorian school yard. Converted from a former bike shed, Rochelle Canteen's wide panel glass doors are opened on warm days, allowing the restaurant to spill into the picturesque surrounding yard. The establishment is the creation of serial caterers and restaurateurs Arnold & Henderson.

Columbia Road French

Brawn

8 49 Columbia Rd
+44 20 7729 5692

brawn.co

⊖ Bethnal Green

Open daily. Mon 6pm-10.30pm; Tue-Thu noon-3pm, 6pm-10.30pm; Fri/Sat noon-3pm, 6pm-11pm; Sun set lunch noon-4pm

Decked out in warm wood and exuding comfort, Brawn specializes in locally sourced delicacies in a wonderfully unfussy setting. The highlight of Columbia Road's many culinary treasures, a meal at Brawn can include such divergent delights as Scottish langoustine, braised rabbit leg, soft polenta and *gremalata*, and the rather more unusual sounding snails, oxtail and salsify pie. Brawn's predominantly French list of sustainable, organic and biodynamic wines is particularly satisfying.

Iberian Flair

Eyre Brothers

9 70 Leonard St
+44 20 7613 5346
eyrebrothers.co.uk
⊖ Old Street
Closed Sun. Open Mon-Fri noon-3pm, 6.30pm-10.45pm; Sat 7pm-10.45pm

Arguably London's best Iberian restaurant, Eyre Brothers melds culinary artistry with a cultivated, contemporary decor. Every element, from the splash of green olive oil bursting with flavour to the stellar wine list, evokes pure pleasure. Muted lighting, modernist wood panelling, tasteful artwork and a buzzing bar add to the restaurant's infinite appeal; but its culinary might is certainly worth multiple visits in of itself.

French Fantaisie

Les Trois Garçons

(10) 1 Club Row
+44 20 7613 1924
lestroisgarcons.com
⊖ Shoreditch High Street,
⊖⊖⊖⊖ Liverpool Street
Closed Sun. Open Mon-Wed
6pm-9.30pm; Thu noon-2pm,
6pm-9.30pm; Fri noon-2pm, 6pm-
10.30pm; Sat 6pm-10.30pm

In the year 2000, the trois garçons Hassan, Michel and Stefan, from Malaysia, France and Sweden respectively, unveiled an over-the-top baroque-chic French restaurant in the former Victorian pub they had already inhabited for four years. Les Trois Garçons takes the Gallic notion of *fantaisie* to new heights. The eclectic, elegant space is adorned with everything from floating vintage handbags and overblown chandeliers to the occasional stuffed beast. Guests choose from a two or three course epicurean prix fixe or opt for the tasting menu.

Factory Floor Dining

Wapping Food

11 Wapping Wall
+44 20 7680 2080
thewappingproject.com
⊖⊖ Shadwell
Open daily. Mon-Fri noon-3.30pm,
6.30pm-11pm; Sat 10am-4pm, 7pm-
11pm; Sun 10am-4pm

Located in the grandiose industrial
Wapping Hydraulic Power Station,
Wapping Food is the culinary
expression of the arts-focused
Wapping Project. The cavernous
space lends itself well to a dramatic
brunch or dinner. Dishes have a
distinctly English bent and include
such mouthwatering classics as
char grilled mackerel, venison pie
and banana and treacle ice cream
for desert.

Oenological Fulfilment

Sager and Wilde

12 193 Hackney Road
sagerandwilde.com

⊖ Hoxton
Open daily. Mon-Sat 5pm to 11pm;
Sun 2pm-11pm

Charlotte and Michael Sager-Wilde's top notch wine bar lights up an otherwise nondescript section of the Hackney Road. The sophisticated oenological selection spans the globe, from California to Jerez. A sturdy assemblage of various meats and cheeses accompany the wines to perfection.

Clerkenwell & Islington

—From Workshop to Urban Loft

Wedged between Bloomsbury and Shoreditch, Clerkenwell was a centre of commerce and manufacturing before it developed into the vibrant urban community it is today. The area is home to some of London's more commercial designers and creative trades, which have turned many of its industrial buildings into lofts spaces.

In the 17th century, the area near the *Clerks' Well*, where London clergymen had performed mystery plays in the Middle Ages, became a fashionable place to live just outside the city gates. The settlement was a popular spa and resort when the Industrial Revolution turned the area turned into a hub for light manufacturing. Clerkenwell also developed a reputation as the print shop for the local left-wing intelligentsia—the Guardian was headquartered in the area until 2008.

Today, much activity is centred on Smithfield Market in the south and Exmouth Market further north along Farringdon Road. While the area around Smithfield Market—still a meat market today—has embraced a distinctly commercial character; pedestrianized Exmouth Market has a more bohemian feel. At the northern edges of the neighbourhood, King's Cross was synonymous with seediness until the Eurostar trains to Paris pulled into nearby St Pancras in 2007.

Islington, the mostly residential neighbourhood north of the Angel, was one of London's first suburbs. The area regained popularity as a place to live in the 1970s when its Georgian terraces where rediscovered by the middle class. Islington is also notorious as the spiritual home of Tony Blair's New Labour.

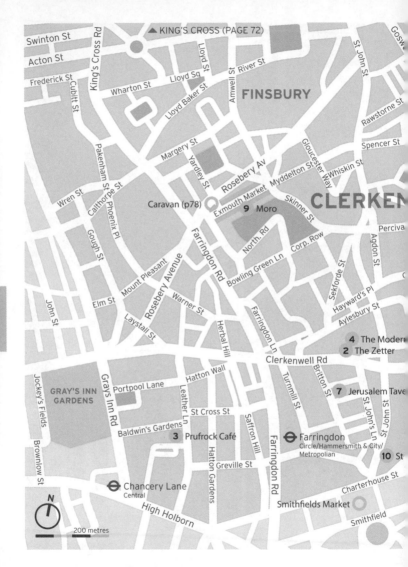

FINSBURY

CLERKEN

Caravan (p78)

9 Moro

4 The Modern
2 The Zetter

7 Jerusalem Tave

3 Prufrock Café

Farringdon
Circle/Hammersmith & City/
Metropolian

10 St

Chancery Lane
Central

GRAY'S INN
GARDENS

Smithfields Market

Smithfield

N

200 metres

Swinton St
Acton St
Frederick St
King's Cross Rd
Cubitt St
Wharton St
Lloyd St
Lloyd Sq
Lloyd Baker St
Amwell St
River St
Pakenham St
Margery St
Yardley St
Rosebery Av
Exmouth Market
Gloucester Way
Myddelton St
Whiskin St
Skinner St
Rawstorne St
Spencer St
Wren St
Calthorpe St
Phoenix Pl
Gough St
North. Rd
Corp. Row
Percival
Agdon St
Sektorde St
Hayward's Pl
Aylesbury St
John St
Mount Pleasant
Rosebery Avenue
Warner St
Farringdon Rd
Bowling Green Ln
Farringdon Ln
Elm St
Laystall St
Herbal Hill
Clerkenwell Rd
Jockey's Fields
Grays Inn Rd
Portpool Lane
Hatton Wall
Leather Ln
St Cross St
Saffron Hill
Turnmill St
Britton St
St John's Ln
St John St
Baldwin's Gardens
Brownlow St
Hatton Gardens
Greville St
Farringdon Rd
Charterhouse St
High Holborn
St John St
Goswe

y St

City Rd

Graham St

Wharf Rd

Wenlock Rd

Taplow St

Bletchley St

Cropley St

Murray Grove

Hall St

Moreland St

Central St

Macclesfield Rd

Micawber St

Wi'sor Terr.

Wellesley Terr.

Shpherdess Walk

Provost St

Nile St

Vestry St

City Rd

Dingley Rd

Dingley Pl

Mora St

LL

Goswell Rd

Lever St

Central St

Ironm'r Row

Cayton St

Bath St

Britannia Walk

Westland Rd

East Rd

Seward St

Radnor St

Peerless St

Pear Tree St

ST LUKES

Bastwick St

rgh St

Gee St

St

Old St

Old St

Old Street
Northern

▶ SHOREDITCH (PAGE 52)

Baltic St

Whitecross St

Banner St

Bunhill Row

Featherstone St

Leonard St

Golden Lane

Dufferin St

Fortune St

City Rd

Tabernacle St

Paul St

Fann St

Bunhill Row

Worship St

rhouse Sq

Barbican
Circle/Hammersmith & City/
Metropolian

Beech St

Lamb's Pass.

Chiswell St

Silk St

Milton St

Finsbury St

Finsbury St

Finsbury Sq

THE CITY

11 Barbican Centre

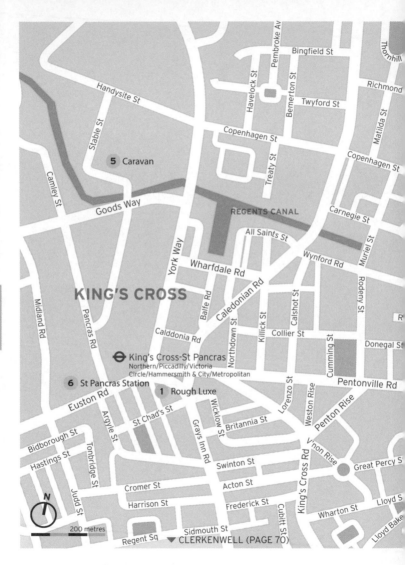

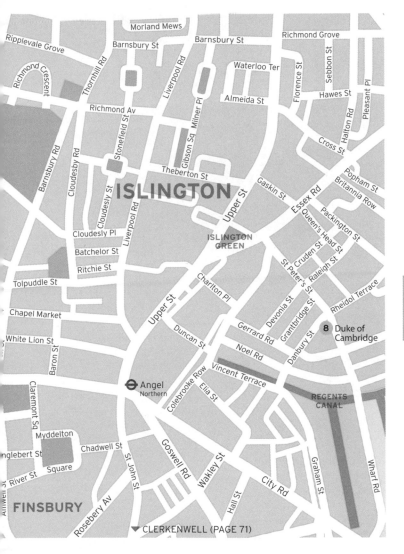

King's Cross Glamour

Rough Luxe

(1) 1 Birkenhead St
+44 20 7837 5338
roughluxe.co.uk
⊖⊖⊖⊖⊖⊖ King's Cross St
Pancras
Doubles from £209/night incl. tax

Rough Luxe merges the luxurious with the rough, creating a uniquely urban hotel environment. The patina of its distressed walls melds seamlessly into such small pleasures as sumptuous bed linen and a special bottle of wine. The decor is warm, hospitable and inviting. A full spread is on offer every morning for breakfast, which can also be enjoyed outside in the bijou courtyard. Cool and shabby chic, the hotel goes beautifully with its up and coming King's Cross surroundings.

Converted Warehouse Hotel

The Zetter

2 86-88 Clerkenwell Rd
+44 20 7324 4444
thezetter.com
⊖ ⊖ ⊖ Farringdon
Doubles from £162/night incl. tax

Housed in a former Victorian warehouse on St John's Square, the Zetter is a sprightly, modern hotel in an attractive historic setting. The lobby bar offers staggering views of the hotel's interior spiral architecture and the on-site Bistrot Bruno Loubet serves meals round the clock. Rooms are similarly pleasant and airy. Halfway between Shoreditch and the West End and close to all of Clerkenwell's attractions, The Zetter's location can't be beat.

Coffee Highlight
Prufrock Café

3 23-25 Leather Lane
+44 20 7404 3597
prufrockcoffee.com
⊖ Chancery Lane,
⊖⊖⊖ Farringdon
Open daily. Mon-Fri 8am-6pm; Sat/
Sun 10am-5pm

For a dose of absolutely stunning coffee in an urban market setting, head straight to Prufrock. In the midst of Leather Lane's mishmash of weekday market stalls and adjacent to the Hatton Gardens Diamond District, this spacious, comfortable café adds a dose of the cutting edge to an otherwise under the radar milieu.

Original Everyday Cuisine

The Modern Pantry

(4) 47-48 St John's Square
+44 20 7553 9210
themodernpantry.co.uk
⊖⊖⊖ Farringdon
Open daily. Mon 8am-11am,
noon-10pm; Tue-Fri 8am-11am,
noon-10.30pm; Sat 9am-4pm,
6pm-10.30pm; Sun 10am-4pm, 6pm-
10pm. Sun/Mon no dinner

Catering to Farringdon's buzzy
media crowd during the week and
delivering a knockout brunch at the
weekend, the Modern Pantry is one
of London's most versatile locavore
kitchens. Sit at listed building's
pretty downstairs café and enjoy
everything from coffee and your
morning pastry to an evening glass
of wine with some light fusion fare,
or opt for the upstairs restaurant for
more serious dining. The signature
sugar-cured New Caledonian prawn
omelette is quite simply not to be
missed.

King's Cross Powerhouse

Caravan

5 1 Granary Square
+44 20 7101 7661
caravankingscross.co.uk
⊖⊖⊖⊖⊖⊖ King's Cross St
Pancras
Open daily. Mon/Tue 8am-10.30pm;
Wed/Thu 8am-11pm; Fri 8am-
midnight; Sat 10am-midnight; Sun
10am-4pm

An Exmouth Market classic,
Caravan's second location in a
cavernous old Granary building at
the core of King's Cross's massive
re-development does spectacular
brunch with a distinct media
buzz. Round the clock, this is the
place to go if you're craving some
of the modern-casual luster of
the antipodes. Caravan doubles
as a coffee roaster, guaranteeing
premium java to refuel even the
weariest of patrons or those just
rolling off the Eurostar from Paris.

Two Hours from Paris

St Pancras Station

6 Euston Rd
+44 20 7843 7688

stpancras.com

⊖⊖⊖⊖⊖⊖ King's Cross St Pancras

Open 24 hours. Hourly departures to Paris, Brussels and the Midlands

St Pancras Station, celebrated for its stunning Victorian architecture, is the destination for Channel tunnel rail services to Paris and beyond. Erected in the mid-19th century as a terminus for the main line to the East Midlands and Yorkshire, the structure only narrowly escaped destruction in the 1960s. The extensive renovations of the early 2000s added a distinct commercial dimension, but its cosmopolitan atmosphere and "Europe's longest champagne bar" make it well worth a visit.

Ancient Tavern

Jerusalem Tavern

7 55 Britton St
+44 20 7490 4281
stpetersbrewery.co.uk
⊖⊖⊖ Farringdon
Closed Sat/Sun. Open Mon-Fri 11am-11pm

The Jerusalem Tavern has moved around the Farringdon area since the 14th century. It has occupied its present, slightly slanted and eminently charming incarnation since 1720. Now owned by Suffolk based St Peter's Brewery, the tavern serves meals in addition to the full range of St Peter's beers and ales. A timeless spot to settle in with a newspaper and a fresh pint of ale while contemporary London whizzes by.

Islington Organic Pub

Duke of Cambridge

8 30 St Peter's St
+44 20 7359 3066

dukeorganic.co.uk

⊖ Angel

Open daily. Mon-Sat noon-11pm;
Sun noon-10.30pm. Lunch Mon-
Sun 12.30pm-5pm. Dinner Mon-Sat
6.30pm-10.30pm; Sun 6.30pm-10pm

A delightful gastropub on a charming Islington street, The Duke of Cambridge was Britain's first certified organic pub. Eighty percent of produce comes from the Home Counties and the menu changes daily according to availability of the freshest seasonal produce. The selection of ales includes two organic examples produced in London itself, not to mention a range of beers, ciders and a wonderful wine list that spans the globe but also includes some exciting English bottles.

Madrid Meets Morocco

Moro

9 34-36 Exmouth Market
+44 20 7833 8336
moro.co.uk
⊖⊖⊖ Farringdon
Open daily. Mon-Sat noon-2.30pm,
6pm-10.30pm; Sun 12.30pm-2.45pm

Award winning Moorish cuisine created by husband and wife team Sam and Sam Clark whizzes out of the open kitchen and onto diner's plates at this Exmouth Market stalwart. The menu remains faithful to pure North African and Spanish recipes, rather than resorting to fusion, and is highlighted by a phenomenal mainly Spanish wine list, including an excellent selection of sherries. Guests can also drop by sister restaurant Morito next door for casual tapas at any time of day.

British Food and Drink

St John

10 26 St John St
+44 20 3301 8069
stjohnrestaurant.com
⊖⊖⊖ Farringdon
Open daily. Mon-Fri noon-3pm, 6pm-11pm; Sat 6pm-11pm; Sun 1pm-3pm

Located in a former Georgian smokehouse, this East London institution is one of the city's premier venues for British cuisine, paired with a superlative wine list. The Smithfield location is cavernous and atmospheric, doubling as a purveyor of fresh bread, wine and cheese. The space's colourful history includes stints as a Chinese beer shop and the headquarters of the publication Marxism Today. Since the restaurant opened in 1994, it has served solely as a bastion of the British culinary arts. The Spitalfields location is equally appetising.

Arts & Architectural Highlight

Barbican Centre

11 Silk St
+44 20 7638 8891
barbican.org.uk
🚇🚇🚇🚇 Moorgate
Daily performances. Refer to website for program

A world-class performing arts complex, the Barbican hosts numerous classical and contemporary music concerts, theatre performances, film screenings and art exhibitions. The Barbican Centre forms part of the eponymous Barbican Estate, an expansive brutalist residential estate built on the rubble of World War II. Both the London Symphony Orchestra and the BBC Symphony Orchestra are based in the centre's Barbican Hall.

South Bank
—Riverside Arts District

South Bank is largely defined by the narrow band of acclaimed entertainment and cultural establishments on the southern banks of the River Thames. Its cosmopolitan qualities have recently been picked up by the more organically evolved locales of Borough and Bermondsey to the east, and South Bank's "string of pearls" is developing into a vibrant riverside neighbourhood in its own right.

The Thames' southern shores had historically lagged London proper in urbanity and sophistication. Over the years, the marshes of the low-lying flood area made way to a patchwork of light industry and working class dwellings. The area saw significant change in the wake of the 1951 Festival of Britain, when the arrival of the Royal Festival Hall redefined its riverside as an arts and entertainment district and the name "South Bank" was formally adopted. The opening of the Tate Modern (p92) in a former power station in 2000 and the extension of the Riverside Walk have stretched the area further down the river, reaching as far as Tower Bridge in the east. South Bank today is a vibrant quarter of bars, theatres and galleries, interspersed with pricey riverside loft living.

Borough, located on the main traffic artery across the Thames into the City of London, is closely associated with its eponymous market. Borough Market, situated under a number of railway arches since the 19th century, is a wholesale and retail food market renowned for the variety of its offerings. The 2013 opening of the Renzo Piano designed Shard of Glass, the tallest sky-scraper in the European Union, complete with luxury hotel, flashy restaurants and swank offices, confirmed the area's ascension out of the mundane. Beyond London Bridge, Bermondsey Street has become the focal point of a refined local restaurant scene.

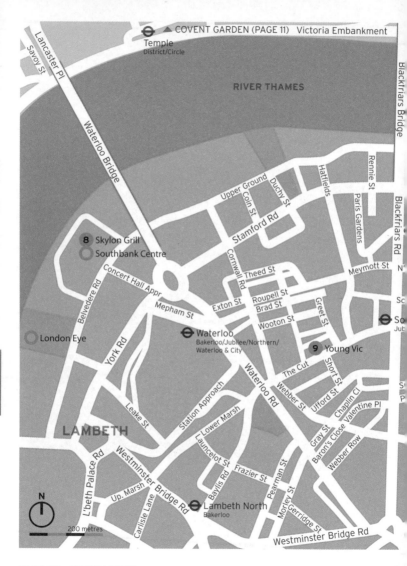

COVENT GARDEN (PAGE 11)   Victoria Embankment

Temple
District/Circle

RIVER THAMES

Blackfriars Bridge

Lancaster Pl

Savoy St

Waterloo Bridge

Upper Ground
Coin St
Duchy St
Stamford Rd
Hatfields
Rennie St
Paris Gardens
Blackfriars Rd

8 Skylon Grill
Southbank Centre

Cornwall Rd
Theed St
Meymott St

Concert Hall Appr
Exton St
Roupell St
Brad St
Greet St

Mepham St
Belvedere Rd
Wooton St

London Eye

York Rd
Waterloo
Bakerloo/Jubilee/Northern/
Waterloo & City

9 Young Vic

The Cut
Short St

Leake St
Station Approach
Waterloo Rd
Webber St
Ufford St
Chaplin Cl
Valentine Pl

LAMBETH
L. Lower Marsh
Gray St
Baron's Close
Webber Row

Launcelot St   Frazier St
Pearman St

Westminster Bridge Rd
Baylis Rd
Morley St
Gerridge St

L'beth Palace Rd
Up. Marsh
Carlisle Lane
Lambeth North
Bakerloo

Westminster Bridge Rd

N
200 metres

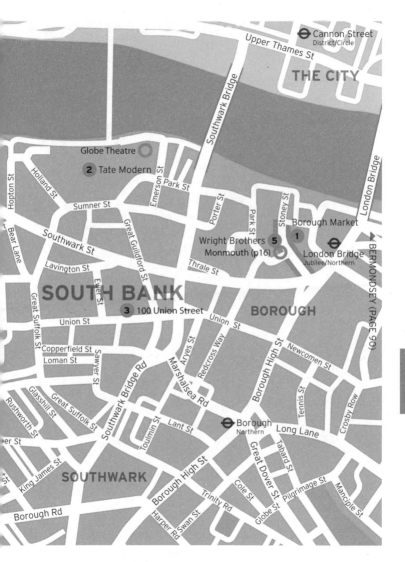

- Cannon Street District/Circle
- Upper Thames St
- THE CITY
- Southwark Bridge
- Globe Theatre
- **2** Tate Modern
- Hopton St
- Holland St
- Emerson St
- Park St
- Porter St
- Park St
- Stoney St
- London Bridge
- Sumner St
- Bear Lane
- Southwark St
- Great Guildford St
- Borough Market
- Wright Brothers **5**
- Monmouth (p16)
- **1**
- London Bridge Jubilee/Northern
- Lavington St
- Thrale St
- Ewer St
- BERMONDSEY (PAGE 90)
- **SOUTH BANK**
- Great Suffolk St
- **3** 100 Union Street
- Union St
- BOROUGH
- Copperfield St
- Loman St
- Sawyer St
- Southwark Bridge Rd
- Aryes St
- Redcross Way
- Union St
- Newcomen St
- Glasshill St
- Great Suffolk St
- Marshalsea Rd
- Borough High St
- Tennis St
- Crosby Row
- Rushworth St
- Toulmin St
- Lant St
- Borough Northern
- Long Lane
- er St
- King James St
- **SOUTHWARK**
- Borough High St
- Great Dover St
- Tabard St
- St
- Trinity Rd
- Cole St
- Globe St
- Pilgrimage St
- Manciple St
- Borough Rd
- Harper Rd
- Swan St

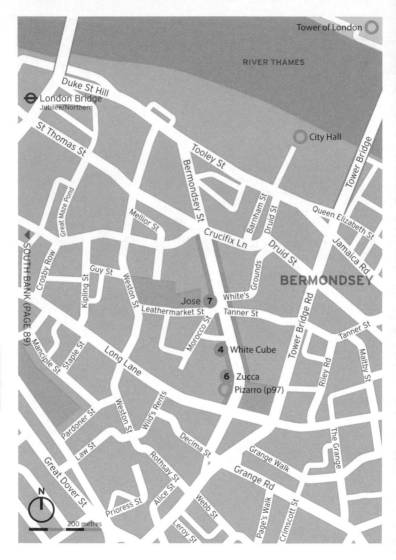

Tower of London

RIVER THAMES

Duke St Hill

London Bridge
Jubilee/Northern

St Thomas St

City Hall

Tooley St

Great Maze Pond

Mellior St

Bermondsey St

Crucifix Ln

Barnham St

Druid St

Druid St

Queen Elizabeth St

Tower Bridge

Jamaica Rd

BERMONDSEY

Crosby Row

Guy St

Weston St

Grounds

Kipling St

Leathermarket St

White's

Jose **7**

Morocco St

Tanner St

Tower Bridge Rd

Tanner St

SOUTH BANK (PAGE 89)

4 White Cube

Riley Rd

Maltby St

Maniple St

Staple St

Long Lane

6 Zucca

Pizarro (p97)

Pardoner St

Weston St

Wild's Rents

Decima St

Grange Walk

The Grange

Law St

Rothsay St

Grange Rd

Page's Walk

Crimscott St

Great Dover St

Prioress St

Alice St

Webb St

Leroy St

N

200 metres

Famous Produce Market

Borough Market

1 Stoney St
+44 20 7407 1002
boroughmarket.org.uk
⊖⊖ London Bridge
Full market open Wed-Sat. Wed/Thu
10am-5pm; Fri 10am-6pm; Sat 8am-
5pm; Mon/Tue lunch only 10am-5pm

London's most celebrated and refined food market dates back to the 13th century when traders were obliged to move here from crowded London Bridge. Borough Market is famously located under a number of railway overpasses, and, since the mid-19th century, beneath an extensive glass and steel roof. A wholesale market to this day, it is renowned for the culinary variety of its retail offerings, such as the Wine Pantry Tasting Room, a purveyor of English wines, and the Wright Bros. Oyster & Porter House (p95).

Modern Art & Design
Tate Modern
2 Bankside
+44 20 7887 8888
tate.org.uk/modern
🚇🚇 Mansion House, 🚇 Southwark
Open daily. Sun-Thu 10am-6pm; Fri/
Sat 10am-10pm
Free admission

Housed in the gargantuan former Bankside Power Station and sitting squarely across the Thames form St Paul's Cathedral, the Tate Modern's setting lives up to its reputation as one of Britain's foremost museums of modern and contemporary art. After contemplating a painting by British icon David Hockney, why not pop upstairs to the restaurant for drinks and some dramatic London views. For more traditional British art, hop on the "Tate to Tate" boat and head over to the Tate Britain across the river.

Pop-up Brownfield

100 Union Street

3 100 Union St
betterbankside.co.uk/buf
⊖ Southwark, ⊖ Borough
Usually during the summer months.
Refer to internet for details

Owned by a local real estate company, this slice of unused urban land adjacent to a rail viaduct has been the site of a series of temporary projects since 2008. Recent iterations included the 2011 Urban Physic Garden (pictured), a collection of medicinal plants and herbs with healing properties, accompanied by workshops and film screenings. In the summer of 2013, the EXYZT collective's "The Lake" featured a shallow boating lake (for inflatable and home-made toy boats), a paddling pool, a juice bar and a long timber deck for sunbathing. Watch this space for upcoming installations.

Cutting Edge Contemporary Art

White Cube

4 144-152 Bermondsey St
+44 20 7930 5373
whitecube.com
⊖⊖ London Bridge, ⊖ Borough
Closed Mon. Open Tue-Sat 10am-6pm; Sun noon-6pm

Cutting edge and controversial contemporary art gallery White Cube's youngest London site speaks volumes about the South Bank's ascent as a cultural and intellectual hub. White Cube has been at the forefront of London's contemporary art scene since the inception of its small Duke Street gallery in 1993. Subsequent iterations, including the (now closed) Hoxton Square gallery curated major works by polemic artists of the Young British Artists movement, the likes of Damien Hirst and Tracey Emin. White Cube's Bermondsey site represents a grown-up phase for the gallery.

Borough Market Oyster House

Wright Bros. Oyster & Porter House

5 11 Stoney St, Borough Market
+44 20 7403 9554
thewrightbrothers.co.uk
⊖⊖ London Bridge
Open daily. Mon-Fri noon-11pm; Sat noon-11pm; Sun noon-10pm

The Wright Brothers oyster and porter bar is one of the highlights of Borough Market. High stools spill over wine barrel tables, and the restaurant's effusive and uplifting vibe is reinforced by the bubbles wafting out of patron's champagne flutes. The freshest seafood is sustainably fished and delivered daily from the shores of Cornwall—Wright Brother's oysters come directly from the restaurant's own Dutchy Oyster Farm on the Helford River.

Stylish Italian

Zucca

6 184 Bermondsey St
+44 20 7378 6809
zuccalondon.com
⊖⊖ London Bridge
Closed Mon. Open Tue-Fri noon-3pm,
6pm-10pm; Sat noon-3.30pm, 6pm-
10pm; Sun noon-4pm

Zucca offers scrumptious modern Italian cuisine in a slick, sophisticated setting. Located at the southern end of Bermondsey Street, the restaurant attracts a buzzing mix of patrons and is very much a part of the revived South Bank scene. Squid nero with white polenta, veal chop with spinach and lemon and other *piati* are accompanied by an extensive Italian wine list.

Sherry Bar

Jose

7 104 Bermondsey St
+44 20 7403 4902
joserestaurant.co.uk
⊖⊖ London Bridge
Open daily. Mon-Sat noon-10.30pm;
Sun noon-5.30pm

A cracking addition to the culinary hotbed of Bermondsey Street, José is a modern Spanish classic. Primarily a bustling sherry and tapas bar, the list of *jerez* is concocted by Masters of Wine associated with the neighbouring Wine and Spirit Education Trust, which ensures a rigorously curated selection. The tapas and deserts, including a highly recommended chocolate mousse, are equally stellar. For those seeking more substantial Spanish fare visit owner José Pizarro's Pizarro (map p90), a wildly successful full-scale Spanish restaurant just down the street.

Thames River Views

Skylon Grill

8 Belvedere Rd
+44 20 7654 7800
skylonrestaurant.co.uk
⊖⊖⊖⊖ Waterloo,
⊖⊖⊖⊖ Embankment
Open daily. Mon-Sat noon-11pm; Sun noon-10.30pm

Perched on the top floor of the Royal Festival Hall, Skylon Grill is the relaxed yet sophisticated *à la carte* section of the more formal Skylon Restaurant. The aesthetic is retro-modernist 1950s and the views of the Thames and the West End cannot be beat. Cuisine is a sublime fusion of Finnish and French, reflected in the decor. The wine list is extensive and excellent. If you are just passing through pre or post-concert, Skylon's bar is a stunning place for a glass of champers.

Sprightly Theatre and Bar

Young Vic

9 66 The Cut
+44 20 7922 2922
youngvic.org
⊖ Southwark, ⊖⊖⊖⊖ Waterloo
Daily performances. Refer to website
for program
The Cut: Closed Sun. Mon-Fri 9am-
11pm; Sat 10am-11pm

The Young Vic hosts excellent
and innovative theatre on its
three stages. Although historically
interconnected with the illustrious
Old Vic theatre down the street, the
Young Vic now operates as a fully
independent venue. A 2004-06
refurbishment won the 2007 RIBA
London Building of the Year award.
The restaurant and upstairs bar,
which spills over onto an outdoor
deck overlooking The Cut, are ever
filled with the buzz of theatrically
charged conversation.

Hampstead & the North

—Bohemian North London Villages

Hampstead, located in the hills of North London, has long held a reputation for the intellectual, liberal and artistic affinities of its residents. Separated from the bustle of London by Hampstead Heath, a hilly expanse of unrestrained parkland, Hampstead shares its laid back and bohemian feel with the nearby "villages" of Golders Green and Highgate.

A spa town since the 18th century, Hampstead saw more development when it was connected to the suburban rail network in the mid-19th century, and especially since 1907 when the newly opened Northern Line provided a fast link to central London. The town attracted a bohemian mix of writers, composers and intellectuals. By the 1920s and 1930s, it had become a hub for avant-garde artists and writers, many of them in exile from Soviet Russia and Nazi Germany. Despite its attraction to the wealthy, Hampstead has maintained much of its bohemian and liberal atmosphere to this day.

The Victorian enclave of Primrose Hill, a charming urban village on the northern fringes of Regent's Park, has a long history as a fashionable and exclusive place to live; the area is notable for its popularity with film and television actors. The adjacent hill, from which the neighbourhood derives its name, offers stunning views over central London.

Nearby Camden Town, although just a few streets away, could not be more different. Located at the junction of several rail lines and the Regent's Canal, its industrial legacy made way for its famous markets and an alternative music scene in the 1970s. More recently, the area has turned into a commercial tourism hotspot.

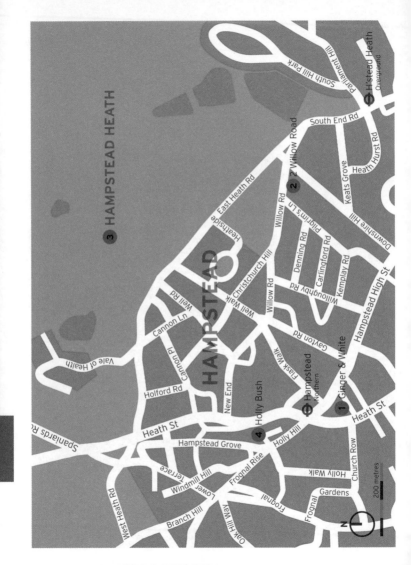

HAMPSTEAD HEATH

HAMPSTEAD

3 HAMPSTEAD HEATH

H'stead Heath
Overground

South End Rd

2 Willow Road

Heath Hurst Rd

Keats Grove

Downshire Hill

South Hill Park

Parliament Hill

Hampstead High St

Kemplay Rd

Carlingford Rd

Denning Rd

Pilgrim's Ln

East Heath Rd

Willow Rd

Willow Rd

Heathside

Christchurch Hill

Well Walk

Willoughby Rd

Gayton Rd

Flask Walk

1 Ginger & White

Hampstead
Northern

Heath St

Church Row

Holly Hill

Holly Walk

Gardens

Frognal

Frognal

Frognal Rise

Hampstead Grove

Lower Terrace

Windmill Hill

West Heath Rd

Oak Hill Way

Branch Hill

Heath St

Hampstead Grove

4 Holly Bush

New End

Holford Rd

Cannon Pl

Cannon Ln

Well Rd

Vale of Health

Spaniards Rd

200 metres

N

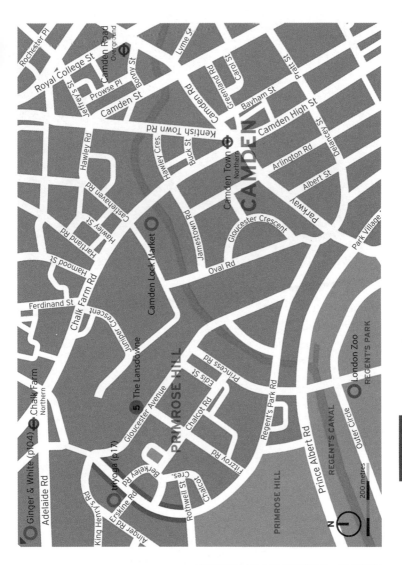

Rochester Pl

Royal College St

Camden Road
Overground

Lyme St

Jeffrey's St

Prowse Pl

Bonny St

Camden St

Greenland Rd

Carol St

Bayham St

Pratt St

Camden St

Camden Rd

Hawley Rd

Kentish Town Rd

Camden High St

Castlehaven Rd

Hawley Cres.

Buck St

Camden Town
Northern

Delancey St

Arlington Rd

CAMDEN

Albert St

Hartland Rd

Hawley St

Jamestown Rd

Parkway

Gloucester Crescent

Camden Lock Market

Oval Rd

Park Village

Hamood St

Chalk Farm Rd

Ferdinand St

Juniper Crescent

PRIMROSE HILL

Princess Rd

Edis St

Regent's Park Rd

London Zoo

REGENT'S PARK

Ginger & White (p104)

Chalk Farm
Northern

5 The Lansdowne

Gloucester Avenue

Chalcot Rd

Fitzroy Rd

Prince Albert Rd

Outer Circle

REGENT'S CANAL

Adelaide Rd

triyoga (p17)

Berkeley Rd

Rothwell St

Chalcot Cres.

PRIMROSE HILL

King Henry's Rd

Ainger Rd

Erskine Rd

200 metres

N

British Coffee Shop

Ginger & White

1 4a-5a Perrins Court
+44 20 7431 9098
gingerandwhite.com
⊖ Hampstead
Open daily. Mon-Fri 7.30am-5.30pm;
Sat/Sun 8.30am-5.30pm

Ginger & White is a top notch "British Coffee Shop" located on a pedestrianised side street in the centre of Hampstead Village. Influenced by the Continent, Australia and New Zealand, the café's owners are nevertheless adamant about their passion for British food, which they serve with aplomb. Ginger & White purveys some of the best coffee in North London—and in a gorgeous setting.

Modernist Home

2 Willow Road

② 2 Willow Road
+44 20 7435 6166
nationaltrust.org.uk/2willowroad
⊖ Hampstead, ⊖ Hampstead Heath
Regular tours. Refer to website for schedule
Admission £6

Built in 1938, the modernist residence at 2 Willow Road was designed as a family home by Hungarian-born architect Ernő Goldfinger. As controversial as it was avant-garde, the house's construction was strongly opposed by a number of local residents, including novelist Ian Fleming, who is said to have used Goldfinger as inspiration for his James Bond villain. 2 Willow Road has luckily seen little change since the 1930s and still contains Goldfinger's innovative furniture and modern art collection.

Heath & Woodland

Hampstead Heath

3 North of East Heath Road
+44 20 7332 3322
⊖ Hampstead, ⊖ Hampstead Heath
Public access

A rambling expanse of heath and ancient woodland, Hampstead Heath lies immediately adjacent to the north and west of Hampstead Village. Long a popular place for leisure and repose for Londoners of all classes, the Heath came into public ownership in 1871 and was thus protected from further development at its edges. Parliament Hill in its southeast corner is one of the highest points in London and offers stunning views of the city's skyline.

Pub on the Hill

The Holly Bush

(4) 22 Holly Mount
+44 20 7435 2892
⊖ Hampstead
Open daily noon-11pm

A glorious little gastropub dating from 1643, The Holly Bush is a jumbly maze of rooms perched high above the rest of Hampstead Village. The Sunday roast is a favourite, but lunch or a pint can be enjoyed here any day of the week. The fireplace and original features, including a creaking winding staircase, allow for some spectacular hop and malt fuelled time travel.

Primrose Hill Pub

The Lansdowne

5 90 Gloucester Av
+44 20 7483 0409
thelansdownepub.co.uk
⊖ Chalk Farm
Open daily. Mon-Fri noon-11pm; Sat
10am-11pm; Sun 10am-10.30pm

A charming gastropub in the thick of Primrose Hill, The Lansdowne is the perfect spot for an afternoon pint or a delicious Mediterranean inspired meal with wine to match. In the colder months, settle at one of the substantial wooden tables by the crackling fire. If it's warm outside, why not take in the bucolic splendour of Primrose Hill while sipping on a glass of rosé from Provence at one of the outdoor tables.

Essentials

Airport Transfer

The fastest way to travel into central London from any of its airports, except for relatively central City Airport, is by train. Taxis are a viable alternative and are readily available at Heathrow and City Airports. A commonly used car service is Addison Lee (addisonlee.com, +44 844 800 6677).

Heathrow (LHR): Heathrow Express train services (£20) connect the airport with Paddington station in central London in 15 minutes, every 15 minutes. A cheaper but slower alternative is the Underground's Piccadilly line (£5.50 at peak, 45 mins) with direct connections to stations throughout central London; trains depart every 5-10 minutes. There is no flat taxi fare to or from Heathrow; fares to the West End are typically £60 or more.

Gatwick (LGW): Gatwick Express train services (£19.90) connect Gatwick with Victoria station in central London in 30 minutes, every 15 minutes.

Stansted (STN): Stansted Express train services (£23.40) connect Stansted with Liverpool Street station in 45 minutes, every 15 minutes.

City Airport (LCY): The airport is directly connected to the Dockland's DLR light rail (£4.50). Taxi rides into the West End cost around £30.

Luton (LTN): Train services (£15) connect Luton Airport Parkway station with St Pancras station in around 30 minutes, every 10 minutes on weekdays. A short bus ride (£1.60) connects the local station to the airport.

Taxis

London's taxi drivers are famously familiar with the city's innumerable small streets and back alleys—in fact, drivers have to pass a test (the "Knowledge") which requires them to know the fastest route between any two streets or points of interest throughout the whole of London.

Quality does come at its price, and fares are in line with those of other expensive northern European capitals. A ride from Notting Hill or Shoreditch into the West End will cost £15 or more and takes around 20 minutes, if

London's notoriously congested streets permit. During rush hour and on weekends, journeys into central London can take significantly longer and the Tube or walking can be a quicker way to get around.

Although some taxis accept credit cards, drivers prefer to receive fares in cash, and payment by credit card is often discouraged through service charges.

Public Transport
The London Underground, also known as the "Tube" given its small diameter, is the oldest underground railway in the world and still provides one of the quickest ways to travel into and within central London.

The Tube operates from around 5.30am until between midnight and 1am, depending on the line, station and day of the week. Trains run fairly frequently, although lines have varying reputations: the Central, Jubilee and Piccadilly lines are reliable and usually run at short intervals, while services on the Circle, District and Hammersmith & City lines can be patchy.

There are six main fare zones. The areas covered in this book are exclusively in Zones 1 and 2. Heathrow Airport is located in Zone 6; City Airport in Zone 3. Ticket prices start at £2 for single journeys within Zone 1. Tickets purchased without using an "Oyster" smartcard, available at all stations and at many newsagents, cost as much as double. "Travelcards" for unlimited travel are available on a daily (£8.40 for Zones 1 and 2), weekly (£29.20) or monthly (£112.20) basis. See p116 for the Tube map.

Tipping
England's tipping culture is fairly reserved—tips are appreciated but not usually expected. Most restaurants add an "optional" 12.5% service charge to the bill which should be honoured in all but exceptional circumstances.

Safety
Although London, like any major city, has its rough patches, its central parts are generally safe. Note that in most areas there is little activity on smaller streets after dark, which makes these more prone to incidents should they occur. Neighbourhoods south and east of central London have historically been less prosperous and safe than those to the north and west.

Index

Credits

Published by Analogue Media, LLC
244 5th Avenue, Suite 2446, New York, NY 10001, United States

Edited by Alana Stone
Layout & Production by Stefan Horn

For more information about the Analogue Guides series, or to find out about availability and purchase information, please visit analogueguides.com

Second Edition 2014
ISBN: 978-0-9912062-0-9

Typefaces: Neutraface 2, Myriad Pro and Interstate
Paper: Munken Lynx

Printed in Barcelona by Agpograf, S.A.

Analogue Media would like to thank all contributing venues, designers, manufacturers, agencies and photographers for their kind permission to reproduce their work in this book.

Cover design by Dustin Wallace
Proofread by John Leisure
Tubemap courtesy of www.london-tubemap.com © Mark Noad

All photography credited to the listed venues unless stated otherwise:
<u>Soho & Covent Garden</u> (9) Stefan Horn (12) Soho House (13/15) Robin Mellor (16) Monmouth Coffee Company (20) Danny Elwes (21) Robin Mellor
<u>Mayfair & Marylebone</u> (27) Stefan Horn (30) David Loftus (32) Jonathan Gregson
<u>Notting Hill & the West</u> (37) Stefan Horn (40) Vencislav Nikolov (41/42) Robin Mellor (43) William Meppem (44) Soho House (45) Robin Mellor (49) © Marcelo Jácome, 2013. Image courtesy of the Saatchi Gallery, London
<u>Shoreditch & the East</u> (51) Alana Stone (55) Soho House (57) Richard Bryant (58) Chris Ridley (59) Andrew Moran (60) Prescott & Conran Ltd (63) Steven Joyce (65) Angus Boulton (66) John Carey
<u>Clerkenwell & Islington</u> (69) Stefan Horn (74) Marcus Peel (76) David Robson (78) Marc Rogoff (79) Robin Mellor (80) St. Peter's Brewery (81) Tricia de Courcy Ling (82) Robin Mellor (83) Laurie Fletcher
<u>Southbank</u> (87) Alana Stone (91/92) Robin Mellor (93) Stefan Horn (94) Photo: Ben Westoby Courtesy White Cube (97) John Carey (98) D&D London (99) Ellie Kurtz
<u>Hampstead & the North</u> (101) Stefan Horn (104) Jonathon Gregson (105) National Trust/David Watson (106) Stefan Horn (107/108) Robin Mellor

About the Series

—A Modern Take on Simple Elegance

Analogue Guides is a series of curated city guidebooks featuring high quality, unique, low key venues—distilled through the lens of the neighbourhood.

Each neighbourhood is complemented by a concise set of sophisticated listings, including restaurants, cafés, bars, hotels and serendipitous finds, all illustrated with photographs. The listings are supplemented by custom designed, user-friendly maps to facilitate navigation of the cityscape. Venues featured in the guides score high on a number of factors, including locally sourced food, tasteful design, a sophisticated and relaxed atmosphere and independent ownership.

Analogue Guides are designed to complement the internet during pre-travel preparation and smartphones for on-the-ground research. Premium photography and a select choice of venues provide an ideal starting point for pre-travel inspiration. At your destination, the guides serve as portable manuals with detailed neighbourhood maps and clear directions.

The result: a compact, efficient, effervescent manual celebrating the ingenuity of the contemporary metropolis.